Breastfeeding

Keep It Simple

FOURTH EDITION

Amy Spangler, MN, RN, IBCLC

Production

Design: Studio Rodrigo, studiorodrigo.com, New York, New York, USA
Photography: Doug Jaeger, dougjaeger.com, New York, New York, USA; Gary
Sloan Studios, garysloan.com, Northborough, Massachusetts, USA; Jensen Larson
Photography, jensenlarson.com, Orlando, Florida, USA
Illustrations: Rick Powell, Montpelier, Vermont, USA
Production Management and Editing: Health Communication Connection, Vienna,
Virginia, USA
Printing: Specialty Lithographing Co., specialtylitho.com, Cincinnati, Ohio, USA

Fourth Edition

19 18 17   2 3 4 5

ISBN 978-1-933634-41-8

For babies everywhere

Learning to breastfeed is like learning to ride a bicycle—
it may seem hard at first, but once you learn, it's easy!

There are a few things you need to know before you begin....

Be patient

Some babies know how to breastfeed right away, but most
need to learn.

Be persistent

It may be several days or several weeks before you and your
baby know just what to do.

Be proud

You are giving your baby a gift that lasts forever.

Table of Contents

Table of Contents

Watch for **bonus videos** and **important tips** throughout this book!

Eager to hear what real moms and dads have to say about breastfeeding? Simply go to the web address next to the video icon.

 View this video to find out more about the baby gooroo video series: **babygooroo.com/resources/videos**

The elephant icon points out information you won't want to forget.

 Ready? Let's go!

Chapter 1
Deciding to Breastfeed

Why should I breastfeed?

Breastfeeding is the way all babies are meant to be fed. It is the safest and simplest way to feed your baby. It makes life easier for the whole family. A healthy, happy baby makes every family member proud!

Breastfed babies are healthier! They have...

- fewer ear infections.
- less gas, constipation, and diarrhea.
- less risk of pneumonia.
- less risk of sudden infant death syndrome (SIDS).
- less risk of obesity in childhood.
- less risk of diabetes.

Breastfed babies are happier! They...

- get to know you right away.
- feel safe in your arms.

Breastfed babies are smarter!
Babies who breastfeed...

- have better brain development.
- do better on IQ tests.

Mothers who breastfeed are healthier!
They have...

- less bleeding after childbirth and lose weight sooner.
- less risk of breast, ovarian, and uterine cancer.
- stronger bones.

Breastfeeding is the safest and simplest way to feed your baby.

Breastfeeding saves time and money! Parents who breastfeed…

- save more than $1,000 (US) the first year alone by not having to buy bottles, nipples, and formula.
- miss fewer days of work.
- lose less income.

Your milk is the only food made just for your baby! Breast milk…

- contains more than 200 nutrients.
- is always ready.
- is clean and safe.
- is never too hot or too cold.
- makes vaccines work better.

Breastfeeding makes your life simpler and easier!

Moms and dads share their breastfeeding advice:
babygooroo.com/resources/videos

What should I do if my family and friends tell me not to breastfeed?

The more you know about breastfeeding, the easier it will be to overlook unhelpful comments from family and friends.

Begin by learning all that you can before your baby is born and sharing this information with those closest to you. Once family and friends understand the many ways breastfeeding benefits you and your baby, they may be more supportive. Let them know that you respect their decisions and you hope that they will respect yours.

Above all, let family and friends know that they are an important part of your life and you hope they will be an important part of your baby's life too.

How can I breastfeed in front of others without feeling uneasy?

Some mothers are uncomfortable breastfeeding in front of others. Some are not. If you live in a place where breasts are seen mostly as sex objects, you may be shy about breastfeeding when others are around. It may help to remember that feeding babies is what breasts are meant to do. With a little practice, you can learn to breastfeed without your breasts showing. Let your partner know that you need his support. Be confident! You are giving your baby the very best.

With a little practice, you can learn to breastfeed without your breasts showing.

Moms share tips on breastfeeding away from home:
babygooroo.com/resources/videos

Will my partner feel left out?

Breastfeeding benefits everyone who is a part of your baby's life. Breastfed babies have fewer sick visits and hospital stays, making parenting easier. Nighttime feedings are simple when there is no formula to mix, measure, or warm. Breastfed babies are portable—good news for families on the go!

Let your partner know how much you need his support as you learn to care for your baby.

Breastfeeding does take time and energy, especially in the early weeks. It is easy for partners—especially fathers—to get discouraged. Fortunately the early weeks are short-lived. Let your partner know how much you need his support as you learn to care for your baby.

Hints for partners, especially fathers

- Learn all you can about breastfeeding.
- Help with positioning, burping, and diapering.
- Feed your partner while she feeds your baby.
- Let your partner know that you are proud of her.
- Spend time alone each day with your baby, go for a walk, splash in the tub, sing, dance, or simply read a book together.
- If you feel jealous or angry, talk about your feelings.
- Spend time alone each week with your partner!

Dads talk about what it's like to have a breastfed baby:
babygooroo.com/resources/videos

Are my breasts too small or too large for me to breastfeed?

Breasts come in all shapes and sizes. Women with small breasts produce just as much milk as women with large breasts. Most babies will learn to breastfeed on their mother's breasts if given the chance. All it takes is practice!

Nipple size and shape can make breastfeeding easier or harder for some babies. If you have questions about the size or shape of your breasts or nipples, talk with your health care provider.

Will breastfeeding change the size and shape of my breasts?

Several things can cause breast size and shape to change, including age, pregnancy, heredity, and weight gain or loss. You may find that your breasts get smaller after your baby is born and the weight that you gained during pregnancy is lost. This can happen no matter how you choose to feed your baby.

Does breastfeeding hurt?

You may feel pulling, tugging, or pain at the start of a feeding when your baby latches on to your breast. If your baby is positioned well, the pain will last only a few seconds. If it lasts more than a few seconds, break the suction by sliding your finger into your baby's mouth. Take your baby off the breast, and try again.

Break the suction by sliding your finger into your baby's mouth.

 Moms share tips on how to know your baby has a good latch: **babygooroo.com/resources/videos**

Ouch! Some moms feel pain when babies latch on, but it should last only a few seconds. If the pain doesn't stop, break the suction by sliding your finger into your baby's mouth. Take your baby off the breast, and try again.

Chapter 2
Getting Ready to Breastfeed

How does the breast make milk?

Grape-like groups of cells inside the breast make milk. These milk-producing cells are called *alveoli*. Small tubes called *milk ducts* carry the milk from the alveoli to openings in the nipple. The small, pimple-like bumps in the *areola*, the darker part of the breast around the nipple, are called *Montgomery's glands*. These glands make an oily substance that protects the nipple.

When your baby breastfeeds, a message is sent to your brain: "I'm hungry!" Your brain hears the message and signals your breasts to release milk. This release of milk is called the *let-down reflex*. You may feel tingling or burning in your breasts when your milk lets down. Or you may see milk dripping from your nipples. Don't worry if you feel or see nothing. Every mother is different.

Your brain also signals your breasts to make more milk to replace the milk your baby takes.

 The more milk your baby removes from your breasts, the more milk you will make.

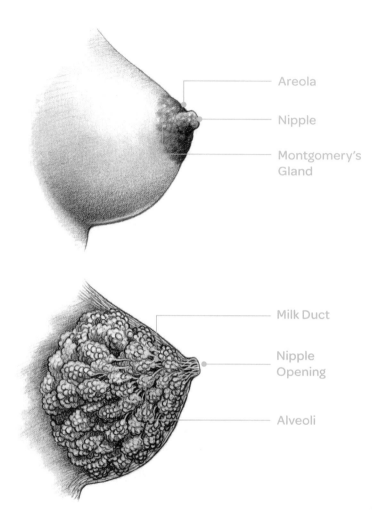

Areola

Nipple

Montgomery's Gland

Milk Duct

Nipple Opening

Alveoli

The human breast has many parts, each with a special role.

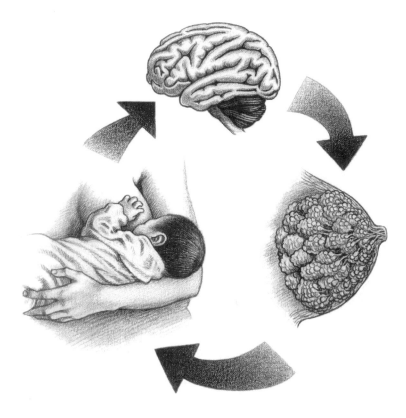

All you need to breastfeed is a breast, a baby, and a brain.

What does human milk look like?

Colostrum is the first milk your breasts will make. It can be thick and yellow or clear and runny. Production of colostrum begins as early as the 16th week of pregnancy and continues for the first few days after birth. New babies need small amounts of food often, so mothers produce small amounts of colostrum each day. Colostrum helps your baby poop, protects your baby from illness, and satisfies your baby's hunger and thirst. Colostrum is your baby's first immunization.

During the first 2 weeks after birth, your milk will gradually change from colostrum to mature milk. Mature milk has two parts, foremilk and hindmilk. Your baby gets foremilk at the start of a feeding and hindmilk at the end of a feeding.

Hindmilk

Foremilk

Foremilk is thin and runny. Hindmilk is thick and creamy. Hindmilk contains more of the fat and calories your baby needs to grow. If you limit the length of breastfeedings, your baby gets little or no hindmilk.

 Colostrum is made just for newborn babies. It provides all the nutrients your baby needs. It may not look like milk, but it is!

How do I care for my breasts?

Breasts and nipples require little or no care. *Montgomery's glands,* small pimple-like bumps in the darker part of the breast around the nipple, produce an oily substance. This substance keeps the nipples moist and helps protect them from infection.

Once you are breastfeeding, follow these simple suggestions....

- Wash your breasts once a day when you bathe or shower.

- Use only clear water and mild soap. Do not use lotions, creams, or oils.

- You do not need to wear a bra while breastfeeding, if a bra isn't something you usually wear. But if you want to wear a bra for comfort or support, you may find a nursing bra handy. Choose a cotton bra that is easy to adjust and fits comfortably. Avoid bras with underwires. If you prefer a bra with an underwire, remove the bra for one or two feedings during the day and at night. This will help ensure that milk is removed from all parts of the breast.

- If you need to wear breast pads inside your bra to protect your clothes, remember to change the pads often. Choose pads made from soft layers of cotton, silk, or wool. Do not use pads with plastic liners that trap wetness. Some pads are made to be used only once; others can be washed and used again.

- If your skin gets dry, you can use a small amount of modified lanolin. A little bit goes a long way.

- If your nipples are tender, put a few drops of breast milk on your nipples and areolas after each breastfeeding.

- If you have painful, cracked, or bleeding nipples, call your health care provider for help!

Avoid using lotions, creams, or oils
on your breasts and nipples.

Chapter 3
Beginning to Breastfeed

How do I get started?

Moms and babies know how to breastfeed—you just don't know you know until you try! Even though breastfeeding may seem hard at first, once you learn, it's easy.

Your baby's first breastfeeding

Hold your baby skin-to-skin between your breasts for at least the first hour after birth. Babies are born with senses and reflexes that help them smell, crawl, lick, latch on, and breast-feed—it's amazing!

Delay less important tasks such as bathing and diapering until your baby has had a chance to get to know you and to breastfeed.

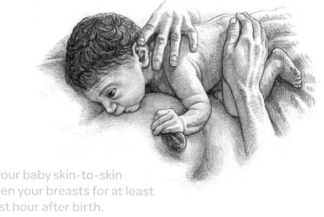

Hold your baby skin-to-skin between your breasts for at least the first hour after birth.

Your baby's next breastfeedings

Keep your baby with you day and night. This is your chance to practice breastfeeding.

Watch for early signs of hunger, and offer your breast at the first sign of hunger. Early signs of hunger include lip-smacking, sucking on fingers or fists, squirming, and fussiness.

Choose a comfortable position. Place your baby on your chest, turn him on his side, or tuck him under your arm so that his head, shoulders, knees, and chest face your breast. Think about how you face the table to eat your meals and position your baby the same way. The best breastfeeding positions are the ones that work for you and your baby.

Support your breast. If you need to support your breast with your hand, make sure you place your thumb and fingers away from the nipple.

Support your baby. Place your thumb and fingers below your baby's ears and around the back of his neck for support. Do not place your hand on the back of his head.

Moms share positioning tips:
babygooroo.com/resources/videos

Cross-cradle
Position

Football
Position

Cradle
Position

Reclining
Position

Sidelying
Position

Choose a comfortable position. Think about how you face the
table to eat your meals and position your baby the same way.

Express (squeeze out) a few drops of colostrum. Place your thumb and fingers opposite one another on the areola, the darker part of the breast around the nipple. Press in against your chest. Then compress (gently squeeze) the breast, not the nipple, between your thumb and fingers.

Tickle your baby's nose with your nipple. When his mouth opens wide, like he is yawning, place him gently on your breast, starting with his chin and lower lip. Make sure he has a good, deep latch and a mouth full of breast!

Hold your baby close and snug. If you hold your baby close, he will be able to latch on well and compress your breast between the roof of his mouth above and his tongue below.

Check your baby's nose, cheeks, chin, and lips. Your baby's chin should press firmly into your breast. His nose and cheeks may lightly touch your breast. His mouth should be opened wide like he is yawning, and his lips should curl out like the lips of a fish!

Moms share tips on how to know your baby has a good latch: **babygooroo.com/resources/videos**

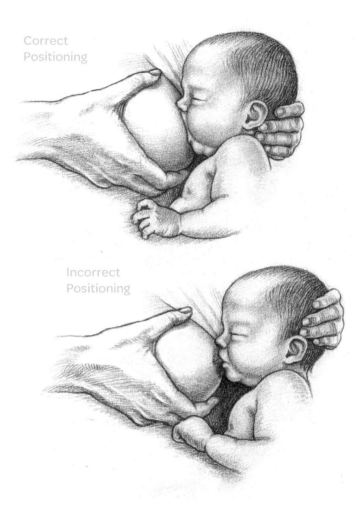

Correct
Positioning

Incorrect
Positioning

Make sure your baby has a good, deep latch and a mouth full of breast!

Watch your baby, not the clock! Breastfeed as long as your baby wishes on the first breast before you offer the second breast. When your baby stops suckling and swallowing or falls asleep, wake him, burp him, and offer the second breast.

Break the suction before you take your baby off the breast. You can break the suction by gently sliding your finger between your baby's gums and into his mouth.

Watch your baby, not the clock!

Offer both breasts at every feeding, but don't worry if your baby seems content with one breast.

Begin each feeding on the breast offered last.

Feed your baby at least eight times in each 24 hours. Frequent feedings give you and your baby a chance to practice breastfeeding.

Avoid bottles and pacifiers. Wait until your baby has learned to breastfeed before you offer him a bottle or pacifier. Bottle nipples and pacifiers can confuse your baby.

Avoid supplements. Your milk has all the nutrients your baby needs. If you give your baby water, formula, or other foods, you will make less milk.

Relax and enjoy this time with your baby!

 Your milk is the only food your baby needs for about the first 6 months.

How often should my baby breastfeed?

Your baby needs to breastfeed at least eight times in each 24 hours. Many babies breastfeed 10 to 12 times a day. Watch your baby for early signs of hunger such as rooting, sucking on fingers or fists, squirming, or fussing. Don't wait for your baby to cry. If you miss the early signs of hunger, or wait for your baby to cry, it can be harder for your baby to latch on and breastfeed well.

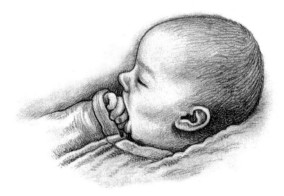

Early signs of hunger include rooting, sucking on fingers or fists, squirming, and fussing.

Some babies breastfeed regularly day and night. Others "cluster-feed," breastfeeding every hour for three to five feedings, then sleeping for several hours in between clusters. Every baby is different. And every day is different! Your baby will let you know when she is hungry. So be sure to keep your baby nearby, so you don't miss her early feeding cues.

Sometimes a sleepy baby will not ask to eat often enough, and you may need to wake her to breastfeed. During the first few weeks, if your baby does not wake to eat at least eight times in each 24 hours, watch for early signs of hunger or light sleep and wake her to breastfeed.

You can be sure your baby is getting enough to eat if she is back to her birth weight by 2 weeks of age and gaining at least 3/4 ounce (20 grams) a day or 5 ounces (140 grams) a week.

Hints for waking a sleepy baby

- Place her in your lap in a sitting position and talk to her.
- Massage her feet and back.
- Remove her diaper.
- Wipe her bottom with a cool washcloth.

 Your baby needs to breastfeed at least eight times in each 24 hours. Many babies breastfeed 10–12 times a day.

How long does a feeding last?

Your baby will let you know when he is full. So watch your baby, not the clock!

Feedings can be short, long, or somewhere in between. How long a feeding lasts depends on whether your baby wants a snack or a four-course meal!

Your baby will let you know when he is full.

When your baby stops suckling and swallowing, burp him and offer the second breast. If he breastfeeds poorly on the first breast, put him back on the first breast before you offer the second breast, so that you can be sure your baby gets the fat and calories he needs to grow. Don't worry if he breastfeeds on only one breast. Each breast can provide a full meal.

Each breast can provide a full meal. So don't worry if your baby breastfeeds on only one breast.

What is the size of an average feeding during the first week?

Your baby needs only small amounts of milk at first. These small, frequent feedings give you and your baby a chance to practice breastfeeding.

During the first day or two, a breastfeeding baby eats about 1–1½ teaspoons of breast milk at each feeding.

By the end of the first week, your baby will be eating about 2–2½ ounces at a feeding.

As your baby grows, so does your milk supply. The more milk your baby takes from your breasts, the more milk you will make.

Day 1
1–1½ teaspoons
(5–7 ml)
at each feeding

Day 3
¾–1¼ ounces
(23–38 ml)
at each feeding

Day 7
2–2½ ounces
(60–75 ml)
at each feeding

How can I tell if my baby is getting enough to eat?

Many mothers worry about whether their baby is getting enough to eat, when in fact making enough milk to fill a baby's tiny stomach is easy. Just remember, nothing comes out the bottom unless something goes in the top! You can be sure your baby is getting enough to eat if she is

- active and alert.
- happy and satisfied after breastfeeding.
- breastfeeding at least eight times in each 24 hours.
- suckling and swallowing while breastfeeding.
- losing no more than 7 percent of her birth weight.
- gaining at least 5 ounces or 140 grams each week after the first week.
- having three or more poops and six or more wet diapers a day by day 5.
- having yellow poop by day 5.
- having clear or pale yellow urine.

If you are unsure whether your baby is getting enough to eat, keep breastfeeding, and call your baby's health care provider or your WIC clinic (see "What is WIC?" p. 118).

 Moms share tips on how to know your baby is hungry: **babygooroo.com/resources/videos**

 Moms share tips on how to tell your baby is getting enough to eat: **babygooroo.com/resources/videos**

What should my baby's stool (poop) look like?

The good news is that breastfed babies' poop doesn't smell bad. The bad news is that there is lots of it!

You will know your baby is getting enough to eat by the color and number of his poops.

Your baby's stool will be

- black, thick, and sticky on days 1 and 2.
- green and pasty by day 3.
- yellow, seedy, and runny by day 5.

After day 2, you should see three or more stools a day. As your baby grows, the number and size of stools will change. After 4 to 6 weeks, some babies will continue to have three or more stools a day. Others will have fewer and larger stools every 1 to 5 days.

 If your baby has black stools on day 3, green stools on day 5, or fewer stools than expected on any day, call your baby's health care provider right away.

DAY	NUMBER	COLOR
1	1+	Black
2	1+	Black
3	3+	Green
4	3+	Green
5	3+	Yellow
6	3+	Yellow
7	3+	Yellow

Number and color of stools during the first week.

Chapter 4
Making Breastfeeding Work

Why does breastfeeding seem so hard at first?

A number of factors can affect how quickly a mother and baby learn to breastfeed. These factors include the baby's age, the mother's use of pain medicine during labor, the type of birth (vaginal or cesarean), the length of labor, the use of instruments during birth (forceps or vacuum extractor), and infection or illness in the mother or baby.

Even when a mother and baby are healthy, learning to breastfeed takes patience and practice. Early, frequent feedings will help you and your baby get off to a good start. As you and your baby grow stronger, breastfeeding will get easier. Soon it will be difficult to remember why breastfeeding ever seemed hard!

Moms share their thoughts on the hardest part of breastfeeding: **babygooroo.com/resources/videos**

Learning to breastfeed takes patience and practice.

How can I breastfeed and still do all the other things I need to do?

In the first weeks after birth, your most important job is caring for your baby and yourself. Leave household chores to others, or if necessary leave chores undone—cobwebs can wait!

The frustrations of parenting seem greater when parents are worn out from too little sleep. So try to nap at least once during the day when your baby naps, and wear your pajamas or nightgown during the first week as a reminder to family and friends that you are still getting your strength back.

Some mothers are comfortable breastfeeding in front of family and friends (both male and female), and some are not. So don't hesitate to speak up if you feel you need more privacy.

It is nice to have help at home, but family and friends can be a source of stress. You or your partner may need to politely explain the benefits of breastfeeding and the importance of frequent feedings, feeding on request, and nighttime feedings. Explain that it is better for you and your baby to nap during the day and breastfeed at night than for Grandma to bottle-feed your baby so that you can sleep through the night.

Eat a variety of healthy foods, and drink to satisfy your thirst. If your urine is clear or pale yellow in color, you will know that you are drinking enough liquids. Use each breastfeeding as a reminder to eat a light snack or drink a beverage.

You can begin light exercise 2–4 weeks after birth, but listen to what your body tells you. Many mothers, eager to lose the weight gained during pregnancy, do too much too soon and quickly regret it. If you have questions about which activities are safe, talk with your health care provider. Remember, these early weeks are a learning experience for the whole family, so relax and enjoy this time together!

Some mothers are comfortable breastfeeding in front of family and friends (both male and female), and some are not.

What should I do if my nipples are sore?

Your nipples may be tender during the first week when you and your baby are learning to breastfeed. Many mothers feel a painful tugging or pulling when their baby latches on to the breast. This is common. If your baby is positioned well, the pain should last only a few seconds. If you feel pain for more than a few seconds, break the suction, remove your baby from the breast, and try again.

Hints for relieving sore nipples

- Begin each feeding on the breast that is least sore. Before your baby latches on, you can start the flow of milk by putting a warm, wet washcloth on the sore breast(s) and doing gentle massage.

- If your breasts are full and hard, express a small amount of milk or colostrum to soften the breast.

- Position your baby correctly on the breast. Remember, his chin should touch your breast and his mouth should be opened wide.

- Hold your baby close to prevent pulling on your nipples. Remember to break the suction before you take your baby off the breast.

- If necessary, breastfeed more often and for shorter periods of time.

- You don't need to wash your nipples before each breast-feeding. Even clear water, used often, will dry the skin.

- After each breastfeeding, put a small amount of breast milk on the areola and nipple of each breast. If your nipples are dry and tender, you might want to use modi-fied lanolin instead. A little bit goes a long way!

- If your nipples are painful, cracked, or bleeding, call your health care provider.

What should I do if my breasts are swollen and hard?

During the first week after your baby is born, your milk supply will steadily increase, and your breasts may feel full and heavy. Frequent breastfeeding will relieve the fullness, but if you delay or miss feedings, your breasts can get swollen, hard, and painful.

Hints for relieving swollen breasts

- Hand express or pump a small amount of milk or colostrum. This will soften the breast and make it easier for your baby to latch on well.

- Use cold packs between feedings to reduce the swelling. You can use bags of frozen peas wrapped in a cool, wet washcloth.

- Increase the flow of milk by gently squeezing your breast when your baby pauses from feeding.

- Breastfeed at least eight times in each 24 hours.

- Wear a bra for comfort and support, but make sure the bra fits well and is not too tight.

After several weeks, your milk supply will change to meet your baby's needs, and your breasts may seem smaller and less full.

Increase the flow of milk by gently squeezing your breast when your baby pauses from feeding.

 Don't worry if your breasts seem less full. You are not losing your milk. Your supply is simply changing to meet your baby's needs.

How can I keep my breasts from leaking?

Leaking sometimes occurs when you think about your baby, hear her or another baby cry, or delay a feeding. Leaking can also occur when you have sex!

Hints to control leaking

- You can stop the flow of milk by pressing the heels of your hands against your nipples or folding your arms across your chest.

- Use breast pads to protect your clothes. Change pads frequently, and do not use pads with plastic liners that trap wetness.

- To hide wetness, choose clothing with light colors and small prints.

- Breastfeed your baby before you have sex.

What are the "baby blues" and how are they different from "postpartum depression"?

After your baby is born, you may find that you feel happy one minute and sad the next. You may even cry for no clear reason. These are signs of the "baby blues." Many mothers experience the baby blues. The symptoms are normal and usually occur 3 to 4 days after birth and last several days.

If your symptoms last longer or get worse, you may have a more serious illness called "postpartum depression." Postpartum depression can occur right after birth, or weeks or months later. Postpartum depression is an illness, not a weakness. Signs of postpartum depression include:

- not wanting to care for your baby or yourself
- loss of appetite
- no energy
- trouble sleeping
- feeling sad or guilty
- feeling anxious or scared
- feeling angry
- having thoughts of hurting yourself or your baby

No one knows what causes postpartum depression, but it may have something to do with the hormone changes that occur during pregnancy and after birth. These hormone changes can cause chemical changes in the brain that lead to depression.

Postpartum depression can last for several weeks or many months. But it's important to know that postpartum depression doesn't last forever. The sooner you get help, the sooner you will start to feel better.

Here are some ideas that other mothers with postpartum depression have found helpful:

- It's okay to feel overwhelmed. Birth brings many changes, and parenting isn't easy.

- Find someone to talk to, and tell that person how you feel.

- Be honest about what you can and can't do, and ask others for help.

- Get help with child care and household chores.

- Do something for yourself each day, even if it's for only 15 minutes. Reading, exercising (walking is good for you and easy to do), taking a bath, or listening to music are some options.

- Accept that you may get only one thing done on some days. There may be days when you can't get anything done. Try not to get angry when this happens.

- Write down your thoughts and feelings each day. Once you begin to feel better, rereading what you wrote will help you see that you are getting better.

- Talk with your health care provider about your feelings. He or she can offer counseling and/or medicines that are safe for you and your baby.

Chapter 5
Taking Care of Your Baby

How do I calm a crying baby?

Babies cry for lots of reasons, and some cry more than others. Sometimes it is easy to know the cause of the crying, but more often no cause is found. Many babies have a fussy period in the late afternoon or early evening. Some babies will stop crying if they are held, cuddled, rocked, or bathed. It takes time to learn how to calm your baby, so be patient.

Begin by checking each of the likely causes. Does your baby have a wet or dirty diaper? Is she hungry, tired, cold, hot, or simply bored? You will soon learn which ways of comforting your baby work best. If the crying continues, your baby may be sick. Check her temperature, and call her health care provider if she has a fever.

There may be times when you are unable to cope with your baby's crying. If this happens, give your baby to someone else to care for or put your baby in a safe place, such as a crib or play yard, and take a break. Do something relaxing like listening to music or taking a bath.

How can I keep my baby safe from SIDS?

Sudden infant death syndrome (SIDS) is the leading cause of death in infants between 1 month and 1 year of age. SIDS occurs most often between 2 and 4 months of age. SIDS is commonly referred to as "cot death" or "crib death" because most SIDS deaths occur while babies are sleeping.

The best way to keep your baby safe from SIDS is to always put your baby on her back to sleep. Never put your baby on her tummy or her side to sleep.

The American Academy of Pediatrics recommends that mothers and babies sleep near one another (in the same room) but not in the same bed. Studies show that when mothers and babies sleep in the same room, nighttime feedings are easier, mothers and babies get more sleep, and babies have a lower risk of SIDS.

More suggestions for keeping your baby safe from SIDS include:

- Breastfeed your baby.

- Place your baby on a firm mattress or other firm surface to sleep. Never put your baby to sleep on a waterbed, sofa, or chair.

- Dress your baby in a single layer of clothing. Don't let your baby get too hot.

- Place your baby in a sleep sack. Even lightweight blankets or covers can trap your baby.

- Don't place pillows, heavy or loose bedding, or stuffed toys in your baby's bed.

- Keep your baby in a smoke-free place. Don't smoke during pregnancy or your baby's first year.

- Take your baby for regular health checks and immunizations.

- Call your baby's health care provider right away if your baby seems sick.

 The American Academy of Pediatrics recommends that mothers and babies sleep near one another but in separate beds.

When will my baby sleep through the night?

After your baby is breastfeeding well and gaining weight, you can begin to let her set her own feeding schedule. This may happen at about 4 weeks after birth. Remember that every baby is different. Some babies will breastfeed every 1–3 hours, day and night, for many weeks. Others will breastfeed every 1–2 hours when awake and sleep for longer periods of time. By 6–12 weeks of age, many babies will sleep from midnight until 4 or 5 o'clock in the morning. You simply need to change your idea of night!

 Breastfeeding your baby and placing her on her back to sleep will help keep her safe from SIDS.

How can I keep my baby from getting a flat head?

Your baby's brain needs room to grow, so his head is made up of soft bones that join together over time. When babies spend a lot of time in one position, a flat spot can form on their heads, and little or no hair may grow on that spot. This condition is called plagiocephaly. Plagiocephaly is a fancy word that means flat head.

Premature babies are more likely to get flat spots on their heads because their heads are even softer than those of full-term babies. Also, premature babies often spend more time on their backs without being moved or held. To prevent a flat head, parents of premature babies are encouraged to hold their babies skin-to-skin against their chest. This is called kangaroo care. (Even full-term babies benefit from kangaroo care.)

 Because the risk of SIDS is greater when babies are on their tummies, never leave your baby alone during tummy time.

Babies who sleep on their backs have less risk for sudden infant death syndrome (SIDS), so you should always place your baby on his back to sleep. You can keep your baby from getting a flat spot on his head by placing him on his stomach when he is awake or carrying him upright in a sling. Tummy time will also strengthen the muscles needed for crawling and sitting. Because the risk of SIDS is greater when babies are on their tummies, never leave your baby alone during tummy time. If you need to leave your baby alone, even for a minute or two, place him on his back. You can put him back on his tummy when you return.

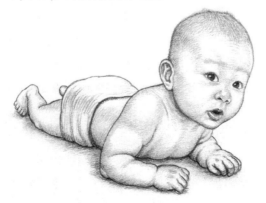

Placing babies on their tummies while awake strengthens the muscles needed for crawling and sitting and helps to prevent a flat head.

Can I give my baby a pacifier?

The more often you breastfeed, the sooner you and your baby will learn this important skill. If you use a pacifier in the early weeks, your baby may breastfeed less often and may not learn to breastfed well. Some studies suggest that use of pacifiers during sleep may reduce the risk of sudden infant death syndrome (SIDS). But it is best to wait until your baby is breastfeeding well (about 2–4 weeks after birth) before offering a pacifier. Many breastfed babies prefer to suck on thumbs, fingers, or fists!

Do I need to give my baby vitamins?

Your baby needs a single dose of vitamin K and a daily dose of vitamin D. Vitamin K is given soon after birth, by your baby's health care provider. Your baby's main source of vitamin D is sunlight. Because the amount of sunlight your baby receives is hard to measure and because too much sunlight can be harmful, many health care providers recommend that babies be given a dose of 400 IU of vitamin D each day beginning soon after birth. Liquid vitamin drops are available at most grocery stores and drugstores. Follow the directions on the package carefully to make sure that your baby gets the right amount of vitamin D each day.

During the last weeks of pregnancy, babies store enough iron in their livers to meet their iron needs for about 6 months. After 6 months, babies get the iron they need from iron-rich foods such as meat and iron-fortified cereal. Your baby's health care provider will let you know if your baby needs iron sooner and may recommend an iron supplement.

When should I give my baby solid foods?

Birth to 6 months

Breast milk is the only food your baby needs for about the first 6 months of life. If you start solid foods too soon, you can cause constipation, diarrhea, gas, or spitting up.

You will know your baby is ready for solid foods if he can sit up, support his head, put food in his mouth, and swallow.

6 months to 1 year

When your baby is about 6 months old, you can begin to offer solid foods. You will know your baby is ready for solid foods if he can sit up, turn his head, put food in his mouth, and swallow.

Even though solid foods provide vitamins and nutrients, breast milk should be a key part of your baby's diet for at least 1 year. If you stop breastfeeding before your baby is 1 year old, ask your baby's health care provider to recommend an iron-rich formula. Your baby should be 1 year old before you give him cow's milk.

 Moms and dads share tips on how to know your baby is ready for solid foods: **babygooroo.com/resources/ videos**

 Your milk is the only food your baby needs for about the first 6 months.

How long should my baby breastfeed?

Some mothers breastfeed for a few weeks, some for a few months, and others for a few years. Any amount of breastfeeding is good for you and your baby. How long you breastfeed depends on your needs and the needs of your child.

Breast milk provides all the nutrients your baby needs for the first 6 months of life. Even after solid foods are introduced, breast milk should still be an important part of your baby's diet. More important than when you wean is that you wean slowly. Some babies wean between the ages of 18 and 24 months. Others continue to breastfeed on and off for 3, 4, or more years—the breast is a wonderful place to eat, sleep, and cuddle!

Hints for weaning slowly

- Replace one breastfeeding at a time with solids or liquids, depending on your baby's age and ability. You might want to ask another family member—perhaps your baby's father, brother, or sister—to offer the substitute.

- Increase cuddling time. Your baby can still find comfort and safety in your arms.

- Keep an active toddler busy with games, outdoor play, and story-telling.

- Expect some milk production for many days or even many weeks after weaning is complete.

Sometimes something happens (accident or illness) and a mother needs to wean quickly.

Hints for weaning quickly

- Hand express or pump a small amount of milk to relieve fullness and prevent swelling. Remove only enough milk to relieve fullness. The more milk you remove, the more milk you will make.

- Put cold packs on your breasts to relieve pain and reduce swelling.

- Wear a snug bra for comfort and support.

- If necessary, your health care provider can suggest pain medication such as acetaminophen (Tylenol) or ibuprofen (Advil).

Some children continue to breastfeed on and off for 3, 4, or more years.

Can I breastfeed if my baby has teeth?

Babies benefit most when they breastfeed for at least a year. Since most babies get their first tooth between 4 and 7 months of age, breastfeeding and teething go hand in hand. Biting can ease the pain of teething, which explains why some babies bite down on any object that finds its way into their mouths— including a mother's breast!

Luckily, babies can't breastfeed and bite at the same time. As long as your nipple is at the back of your baby's mouth (away from his teeth), you don't need to worry about biting. If biting does occur, it is usually at the end of a feeding when your baby is full. So watch for signs of fullness and remove your baby from your breast before he has a chance to bite.

More suggestions for preventing biting include:

- Offer your baby a soother before you breastfeed. A cold, wet washcloth or a rubber teething ring can soothe painful gums. Babies 6 months or older who are eating solid foods may find cold foods soothing. Try applesauce, yogurt, or a frozen banana.

- Check your baby's latch. A baby who is latched on well can't bite.

- Give your baby your full attention. Some babies bite when mom's attention is elsewhere. Limit distractions by turning off the TV, dimming the lights, or moving to a quiet room.

Should your baby bite, try to resist the temptation to push your baby away and gently press his face into your breast instead for a second or two. When he releases your nipple to breathe, remove him from the breast and firmly say "no." If the biting continues, put your baby in a safe place, wait several minutes, then try once more to complete the feeding. Your baby will soon learn that biting brings an end to breastfeeding, and the biting will stop. Like other stages in your baby's life, biting will soon become a thing of the past.

Moms share tips on breastfeeding a baby who has teeth:
babygooroo.com/resources/videos

What are growth spurts?

There may be times when your baby grows faster than usual. This is called a growth spurt. A sudden increase in the number of breastfeedings may signal a growth spurt. Growth spurts often occur around 3 weeks, 6 weeks, 3 months, and 6 months. But growth spurts can occur at any time. Because your baby wants to eat all the time, your family and friends may suggest that "you are not making enough milk," that "you need to give your baby solid foods or formula," or that "it is time to stop breastfeeding." Be patient. After 2–3 days, your milk supply will increase and your baby will ask to breastfeed less often.

What are nursing strikes?

A nursing strike is a sudden refusal to breastfeed. Sometimes the strike has a clear cause such as teething, fever, ear infection, stuffy nose (cold), constipation, or diarrhea. Deodorant, perfume, or powder placed on a mother's skin can also cause a strike. Sometimes no cause is found.

If you experience a nursing strike, you will need to hand express or pump your breasts until the strike ends. In the meantime, give your baby your expressed milk using a teaspoon, eye dropper, hollow-handled medicine spoon, or cup. Watch your baby for early signs of hunger and offer the breast at those times. Breastfeed in a quiet place. Give your baby your full attention. Last but not least, don't panic! Nursing strikes seldom lead to weaning.

Chapter 6
Breastfeeding Special Babies

Can I breastfeed if I have more than one baby?

Many mothers produce enough milk to meet the needs of two (or more) babies. The more milk your babies take from your breasts, the more milk you will make.

At first you may find it easier to feed one baby at a time. But after you and your babies have learned to breastfeed well, you can save time by feeding two babies at once. Some babies will breastfeed on one breast at a feeding, while others will breastfeed on both breasts. Just remember that each baby needs to breastfeed at least eight times in each 24 hours.

Two or more babies take more time no matter how you choose to feed them. So don't forget to take care of yourself as well as your babies. Eat a variety of healthy foods, drink enough fluid to satisfy your thirst, and accept offers of help from family and friends.

Breastfeeding two babies at once saves time and energy.

Can I breastfeed if my baby is born early?

The birth of a tiny baby born weeks or months early can be scary. You may have many questions.

- Why did this happen?
- Was it something I did?
- How will she eat if she is too little to suck?
- Can I breastfeed?

Babies born early can be breastfed, even those needing special care. Breastfeeding gives parents a chance to share in the care of their baby and to do something that no one else can do. The milk of mothers who give birth early contains just the right amount of nutrients to meet the needs of even the earliest babies.

Let the hospital staff know that you plan to breastfeed. If your baby is too small or too sick to breastfeed, she can still be fed your milk. The hospital staff can show you how to express and store your milk.

As soon as your baby is well enough to be held for a period of time each day, ask her nurse if you or your partner can put her underneath your clothing and cuddle her skin-to-skin against your chest (kangaroo care).

Your baby's health care provider will let you know when your baby is ready to breastfeed.

Babies held skin-to-skin breathe more evenly, gain weight faster, go home from the hospital sooner, and are more likely to breastfeed.

Can I breastfeed if I have a cesarean birth?

Mothers who have had a cesarean birth can still breastfeed. If the mother or baby needs special care, the start of breastfeeding may be delayed. If you have had a cesarean birth, you may find the following suggestions helpful.

- Choose a comfortable position. Use extra pillows to protect the incision (cut) and provide support. The side-lying or football positions are best.

- Keep your baby in the room with you to save time and energy.

- Get plenty of rest. Nap when your baby naps.

- Limit your activity. Try not to do any heavy lifting, household chores, or brisk exercise for 4–6 weeks.

- Pain medicine may be necessary for several days. Your health care provider will recommend medicine that is safe for you and your baby.

Choose a comfortable position, using extra
pillows to protect the incision.

Chapter 7
Taking Care of Yourself

Do I need to change what I eat?

You can eat all the foods you ate before! Choose a variety of foods—vegetables, fruits, meat, poultry, fish, beans, eggs, yogurt, milk, cheese, and whole-grain bread, cereal, rice, and pasta. Drink enough liquids so that you are not thirsty. Water, nonfat or low-fat milk, and unsweetened fruit juice are good choices. You will know that you are drinking enough liquids if your urine is clear or pale yellow in color.

Some mothers find that certain foods make their baby fussy. If this happens, simply stay away from those foods.

Eat a variety of foods—vegetables, fruits, meat, poultry, fish, beans, eggs, yogurt, milk, cheese, and whole-grain bread, cereal, rice, and pasta.

Can I breastfeed and still lose weight?

Mothers who breastfeed often lose weight more easily than mothers who don't. This happens because some of the calories needed to make breast milk come from the fat stored during pregnancy. The rest of the calories come from the foods you eat. Remember to eat a variety of healthy foods each day (vegetables, fruits, whole-grain breads and cereals, meat, fish, poultry, eggs, milk, and cheese) and to exercise regularly.

To lose added pounds...

- drink nonfat or low-fat milk, water, or unsweetened fruit juice.
- eat fewer sweets such as cookies, candy, cake, pie, and ice cream.
- snack on fresh fruits and raw vegetables.
- bake or broil meat and fish.
- exercise each day (walking, biking, running).

Can I drink alcohol?

Alcohol (beer, wine, liquor) passes easily into breast milk, and
even small amounts can affect your ability to care for your
baby. If you choose to drink alcohol, have no more than one
or two drinks a week and wait at least 2 hours after you drink
before breastfeeding.

Can I smoke or chew tobacco?

Smoke and nicotine can harm not only you but also your baby. Babies who live with smokers (moms, dads, grandparents, etc.) are more likely to get ear infections, pneumonia, and asthma. They are also more likely to suffer from sudden infant death syndrome (SIDS). The more cigarettes you or a member of your household smoke, the greater your baby's health risks.

For breastfeeding mothers, smoking has been linked to lower milk production and earlier weaning, although the exact cause is unclear. If you smoke or chew tobacco and cannot stop, you should still breastfeed. Breast milk may counteract some of the negative effects of cigarette smoke, so it's better to smoke fewer cigarettes and breastfeed than to formula-feed.

To limit your baby's exposure to the toxic chemicals in cigarettes, keep an extra-large shirt handy and put it on over your clothing whenever you smoke. Wash your hands after smoking and before holding your baby. Don't smoke or allow others to smoke in your house or car or near your baby.

Can I breastfeed if I take "street" drugs?

Drugs that are sold on the street (crack, heroin, marijuana, and methamphetamine) can harm you and your baby. Street drugs pass into your milk and to your baby. They can make it hard for your baby to eat, sleep, breathe, and grow. Mothers who take street drugs should not breastfeed.

What if I get sick and need medicine?

Unless you have a serious illness like HIV/AIDS, the best protection for your baby is your milk, so keep breastfeeding.

Check with your health care provider before you take any medicine, including medicine you buy over the counter (without a prescription). Make sure your health care provider knows that you are breastfeeding, so he or she can recommend medicine that is safe for you and your baby.

Take care of yourself and your baby. Keep your baby in the room with you and nap when he naps. Ask family and friends to help with household chores.

If you have to stay in the hospital, let the hospital staff know that you are breastfeeding and ask if your baby can stay with you.

If you need to be away from your baby, you can hand express or pump your breasts to relieve fullness and to keep your milk supply. The hospital or WIC clinic may have a breast pump that you can use (see "What is WIC?" p. 118). Most babies will breastfeed again when given the chance. If your baby refuses to breastfeed, ask your health care provider for help.

How will breastfeeding affect my sex life?

You may have little interest in sex at first. A new baby takes time and energy. Many women worry that sex will be painful or that they will get pregnant again. Let your partner know how you feel.

Before you have sex, talk with your health care provider about birth control and choose a method that fits your lifestyle.

When you have sex, milk can leak from your breasts. It will help if you breastfeed your baby before you make love. This will give you more time for sex or sleep, whichever comes first!

When you breastfeed, your vagina (birth canal) may be dry, and sex can be uncomfortable. A water-based lubricant can be helpful. Put a small amount around the opening of the vagina before having sex.

Can I take birth control pills while I am breastfeeding?

Birth control pills that contain estrogen can decrease your milk supply, but birth control pills that contain only progesterone are thought to be safe. Some mothers notice a decrease in their milk supply even when taking progesterone-only pills. So it is best to wait until you have a good supply of milk (at least 6 weeks after your baby is born) before taking pills that contain progesterone.

If you notice a decrease in your milk supply after starting progesterone-only pills, talk with your health care provider about another type of birth control. There are many choices, including natural family planning, diaphragm, sponge, vaginal ring, intrauterine device (IUD), condom, and spermicidal cream, foam, or gel.

Can I get pregnant if I am breastfeeding?

It's true that a mother who breastfeeds fully and never—or almost never—gives her baby formula, water, or other foods is less likely to get pregnant. In fact, many women worldwide rely on breastfeeding as a short-term method of birth control. It is known as the Lactational Amenorrhea Method (LAM). In order for LAM to be effective, however, both you and your baby must meet certain requirements.

Your baby must be less than 6 months old and breastfeeding fully (exclusively) during the day and at night. And you must not have resumed menstruation (monthly bleeding).

Any behavior that reduces the amount of time your baby spends at the breast, such as use of formula, water, or other foods, frequent pacifier use, or long periods of uninterrupted sleep, increases your pregnancy risk. If you do not want to have another baby soon, talk with your health care provider about birth control.

If I get pregnant, can I still breastfeed?

Many mothers continue to breastfeed an older baby while pregnant, and some older babies continue to breastfeed after the new baby is born. This is called "tandem nursing." In order to meet the nutritional needs of two babies as well as your own needs, eat a variety of healthy foods, drink to satisfy your thirst, and nap when your babies nap.

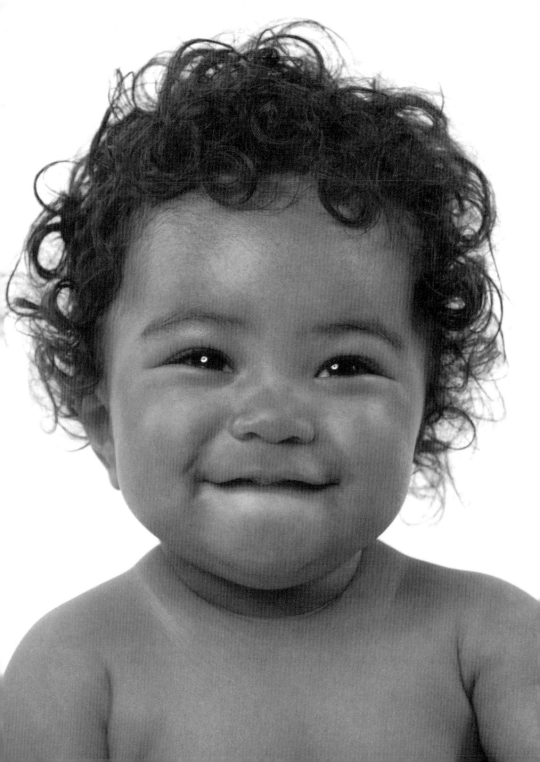

Chapter 8
Returning to Work or School

Can I breastfeed after I go back to work or school?

Many mothers continue to breastfeed after they return to work or school. It takes a little extra planning, but the benefits are worth it!

- Breastfeeding keeps you and your baby close even when you are apart.
- Breastfed babies are healthier, even those in child care.
- Mothers who breastfeed miss less work and lose less income.
- Breastfeeding saves time with no formula to mix, measure, or warm.
- Breastfeeding makes parents' lives simpler, especially for parents going back to work or school.

Learn how to express and collect your milk

If you plan to have your milk fed to your baby while you are apart, you will need to learn how to express and collect your milk. Practice early and often so that you learn this important skill before you return to work or school.

If you plan to have your milk fed to your baby while you are apart, you will need to learn how to express and collect your milk.

Decide who will take care of your baby

Choose a child care provider who...

- provides a safe, clean place for your baby.
- understands and supports breastfeeding.
- has taken care of breastfed babies before or is willing to learn.
- is near your work or school if you wish to breastfeed during the day.

Introduce a bottle or cup

If you are going to be away from your baby during feeding times, you need to know that she will accept food from something other than the breast and from someone other than you. About 2 weeks before you return to work, offer your baby your milk in a bottle or cup. (Babies can learn to cup feed at any age.)

If you use a bottle, try different kinds of nipples until you find one that your baby will take. You may find it easier if someone other than you offers your expressed milk.

Parents who breastfeed miss less work and lose less income.

Breastfeeding saves time with no formula to mix, measure, or warm.

How do I express my milk?

You can express your milk by hand or with a pump. If you will
need to express often or for many weeks or months, you can
rent or buy an electric pump with a special kit that lets you
pump both breasts at the same time.

You can rent or buy an electric pump
with a special kit that lets you pump
both breasts at the same time.

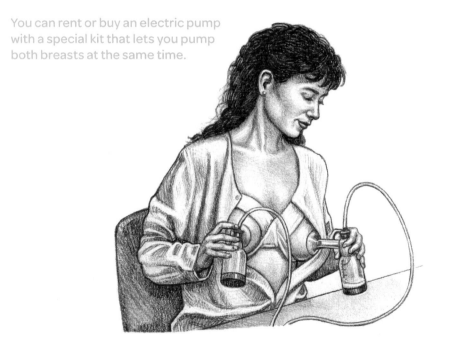

At first, you may get only enough milk to cover the bottom of the collection container. Don't worry! It may take several days before you see an increase in the amount of milk expressed. Try to relax and think about your baby.

Hints for expressing your milk with a pump

You can express milk from one breast while your baby breast-feeds from the other breast, or you can express milk between feedings. When your baby breastfeeds, a let-down reflex occurs. Mothers who pump while breastfeeding often get more milk.

Mothers who pump while breastfeeding often get more milk.

If your baby is unable to keep up with the added flow of milk, he will pull away from the breast for several seconds until the flow slows down. You may want to keep a cloth handy to catch the sprays!

- Before you start, wash your hands with soap and water and rinse well.

- Follow the directions that come with your pump.

- Express for 5–10 minutes or until the flow of milk slows down. Rest for 3–5 minutes, and then repeat once or twice.

- Express each breast until the flow of milk slows down and the breast softens.

- Wash the pump parts after each use in hot, soapy water and rinse well.

- At work or school, rinse the pump parts in hot water. Wash in hot, soapy water when you get home.

Hints for expressing your milk by hand

- Use a clean glass container with a wide opening.

- Press your breast against your chest, and then gently squeeze your breast between your thumb and fingers.

- Move your thumb and fingers around the breast until all parts of the breast are soft and the flow of milk slows down.

Hints to make expression easier

- Choose a quiet, comfortable place.
- Put warm, wet washcloths on your breasts.
- Massage your breasts in a circular motion.
- Relax and think about your baby.
- Listen to relaxing music or soothing sounds.
- Look at a picture of your baby.
- Eat a healthy snack.

Press your breast against your chest, and then gently squeeze your breast between your thumb and fingers.

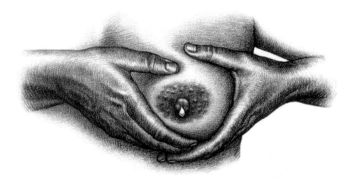

You can store your milk in any container made for food. Use something that is not likely to break, tear, or tip over in the refrigerator or freezer. There are even plastic storage bags made just for breast milk. Place the container of milk in a refrigerator or freezer, or store it in a thermos or cooler.

A special bra allows a mother to pump hands-free.

How do I choose a breast pump?

Many different types of pumps are available:

- manual (hand) pumps
- battery-operated pumps
- semi-automatic electric pumps
- automatic (self-cycling) electric pumps

Whether you plan to pump two or three times a day or two or three times a week, you should choose a pump that is comfortable and easy to use. The pump should provide gentle compression of the breast and removal of milk with the least amount of vacuum. Milk expression should be quick, easy, and painless! Important features include adjustable vacuum, back-flow protection, and double-pumping capability. The more expensive pumps are available for sale or rent.

You may want to wait until after your baby is born to buy or rent a breast pump, just in case plans made during pregnancy change. Here are some things to consider when choosing a breast pump....

- Why do you need a breast pump?
- How often do you plan to pump?
- Is the pump comfortable?
- Is the pump easy to use?
- Is the pump easy to clean?
- How much does the pump cost?

Manual (hand) pumps are designed for mothers who need to pump now and then.

Fully automatic pumps that let you pump both breasts at the same time are designed for mothers who need to pump every day.

How long can I store my milk?

Handle your breast milk the same way you care for other foods. Store your milk in a cool place, refrigerate it as soon as possible, and freeze it for later use. If you are storing milk for a healthy, full-term baby, follow these simple suggestions.

- Store your milk in any container made for food. Label the container with your name, your baby's name, the date, and the time.

- Place a single serving in each container. Allow room for expansion, if you plan to freeze your milk.

- Store your milk in the center of the refrigerator or freezer, away from the door.

Store your milk in any container made for food.

- Studies show that milk collected under ideal conditions (clean and cool) can be stored for up to 8 hours in a cool room, 8 days in a refrigerator, and 12 months in a freezer.

- Many times, however, conditions may not be ideal. To be safe, store your milk in a cool room for up to 5 hours, in a refrigerator for up to 5 days, or in a freezer for up to 5 months.

- If you forget storage times, simply count the number of fingers on one hand as a reminder—five!

Room
Up to 5 hours at 85°F
(29°C) or cooler

Freezer
Up to 5 months at 0°F
(-18°C) or cooler

Refrigerator
Up to 5 days at 39°F
(4°C) or cooler

Breast milk storage guidelines for healthy, full-term babies.

- To thaw, place the unopened container in the refrigerator or in a pan of warm water.

- Do not thaw or warm any milk for your baby in a micro-wave oven. A microwave oven destroys live cells and heats the milk unevenly. Although a few drops of milk on your wrist or arm may not feel hot, portions of the milk may be hot. Hot milk can burn your baby.

- Milk that has been thawed in the refrigerator should be used within 24 hours. Milk that has been thawed in a pan of warm water should be used right away or stored in the refrigerator for up to 4 hours.

BREAST MILK	ROOM 85°F (29°C) OR COOLER	REFRIGERATOR 39°F (4°C) OR COOLER	FREEZER 0°F (-18°C) OR COOLER
FRESH	Use within 5 hours	Use within 5 days	Use within 5 months
PREVIOUSLY FROZEN, THEN THAWED IN REFRIGERATOR	Use within 4 hours	Use within 24 hours	Do not refreeze
PREVIOUSLY FROZEN, THEN THAWED IN WARM WATER	Use right away	Use within 4 hours	Do not refreeze

Guidelines for using stored breast milk.

- Breast milk is easy to prepare. No heating is needed. Simply remove the milk from the refrigerator and serve. If your baby prefers milk at room temperature, place the unopened container in a pan of warm water for several minutes.

- Any milk left in the feeding container (e.g., bottle or cup) can be refrigerated and used within 1 hour to finish the feeding.

Chapter 9
Finding Help

Where can I find help with breastfeeding?

There are many health professionals to whom you can turn for help, including WIC nutritionists, International Board Certified Lactation Consultants, La Leche League Leaders, and breastfeeding peer counselors. Family and friends who have breastfed can also be a source of much-needed encouragement and support. If you or your baby has a medical problem, contact your health care provider or your baby's health care provider right away.

Moms share tips on where to find help:
babygooroo.com/resources/videos

Family and friends who have breastfed can be a source
of much-needed encouragement and support.

What is WIC?

WIC (the Special Supplemental Nutrition Program for Women, Infants and Children) is a special government program that provides healthy foods and nutrition counseling to low-income women who are pregnant, have recently given birth, or are breastfeeding, and to children up to age 5 years.

More than 50 percent of babies born in the United States participate in WIC. WIC nutritionists, nurses, and peer counselors serve between 7 and 8 million women and children each month.

How do I qualify for WIC?

Your income must be below a certain level, you must meet the residency requirements of the state or Indian Tribal Organization where you apply, you must qualify for one of the categories served by WIC (pregnant women, postpartum breastfeeding women, postpartum nonbreastfeeding women, infants, and children up to 5 years of age), you must live in an area that has a WIC clinic, and a health professional must confirm that you are at "nutritional risk."

If your income allows you to participate in programs such as the Supplemental Nutrition Assistance Program (SNAP), Medicaid, or Temporary Assistance to Needy Families (TANF), you meet the income requirements for WIC. But you must also meet the residency requirement and be at nutritional risk to qualify for WIC.

What foods does WIC provide?

WIC food packages now include foods such as tortillas, brown rice, oatmeal, soy-based drinks, canned salmon, lentils, and tofu that appeal to families from a variety of cultural backgrounds.

To ensure that WIC moms and babies have a healthy diet—low in fat and sugar, and high in fiber—WIC also provides a variety of approved foods, including fresh and frozen fruits and vege-tables, eggs, milk, cheese, whole-grain bread and cereal, peanut butter, beans, peas, infant formula, and baby fruits, vegetables, meats, and cereal.

WIC supports breastfeeding by giving fully breastfeeding mothers more food, including fruits and vegetables and certain types of canned fish, and by giving breastfed babies more baby fruits, vegetables, and meats.

How does WIC help breastfeeding mothers?

WIC helps breastfeeding mothers and babies in many ways.

- Women who breastfeed can participate in WIC until their babies are 1 year of age. Women who formula-feed can participate only until their babies are 6 months of age.

- Women who breastfeed receive more foods for themselves and their children.

- Knowing that breastfeeding is the best choice for babies, WIC staff encourage and support breastfeeding.

- Some WIC clinics employ lactation consultants and peer counselors who provide breastfeeding support during and after pregnancy.

- Some WIC clinics provide breast pumps so that mothers can continue to breastfeed after returning to work or school.

To find a WIC clinic in your area, check with your local health department or contact...

USDA Food and Nutrition Service

WIC
Tel: (703) 305-2746
Website: www.fns.usda.gov/wic/women-infants-and-children-wic

Women who breastfeed receive more food for themselves and their families.

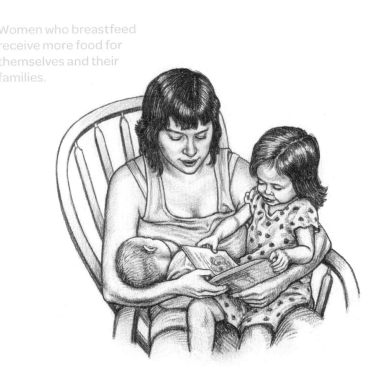

What is an International Board Certified Lactation Consultant?

An International Board Certified Lactation Consultant (IBCLC) is a health care provider with special knowledge and skills in breastfeeding management. To become an IBCLC, an individual must pass a test given by the International Board of Lactation Consultant Examiners. IBCLCs work in hospitals, WIC clinics, and health care providers' offices, and in private practice. An IBCLC can give you confidence in your ability to breastfeed and help you manage any problems that may occur.

To find an International Board Certified Lactation Consultant (IBCLC) in your area, contact...

International Lactation Consultant Association

2501 Aerial Center Parkway, Suite 103
Morrisville, NC 27560

Tel: (888) 452-2478
Email: info@ilca.org
Website: ilca.org

What is a La Leche League Leader?

A La Leche League Leader is an experienced mother who has breastfed her own children for at least 1 year and who has been trained to answer your breastfeeding questions. To become a La Leche League Leader, an individual must be accredited by La Leche League International, an organization with the sole purpose of helping mothers breastfeed. La Leche League Leaders are representatives of La Leche League International and serve as volunteers.

To find a La Leche League Leader in your area, contact...

La Leche League International
350 E. Wacker Drive, Suite 85
Chicago, IL 60601

Tel: (800) 525-3243
Website: llli.org

What is a breastfeeding peer counselor?

A breastfeeding peer counselor is a mother who has breast-fed her own children and helps mothers in her community breastfeed. To become a breastfeeding peer counselor, an individual must complete a breastfeeding peer counselor training program. Breastfeeding peer counselors may work as volunteers or be paid by an agency.

To find a breastfeeding peer counselor in your area, contact your local hospital, health department, or WIC clinic.

Moms and dads share their breastfeeding advice:
babygooroo.com/resources/videos

What does that word mean?

Alveoli

Alveoli are groups of cells inside the breast that make milk.

Areola

The areola is the darker part of the breast around the nipple.

Colostrum

Colostrum is the first milk your breasts make.

Let-down reflex

The release of milk from the breast is called the let-down reflex.

Milk duct

Milk ducts are small tubes that carry milk from the milk-producing cells (alveoli) to the openings in the nipple.

Montgomery's gland

Montgomery's glands are small, pimple-like bumps in the darker part of the breast around the nipple (areola).

Index

Amy Spangler, MN, RN, IBCLC, is a wife, mother, nurse, lactation consultant, educator, and author. She earned her bachelor's degree in nursing from The Ohio State University and her master's degree in maternal and infant health from the University of Florida. Amy is a registered nurse, an International Board Certified Lactation Consultant, a former president of the International Lactation Consultant Association, and a former chair of the United States Breastfeeding Committee. Amy has worked with mothers, babies, and families for over 30 years. She and her husband live in Atlanta, Georgia. They have two sons and one grandson.

For more information about
our products, please contact:

baby gooroo
P.O. Box 501046
Atlanta, GA 31150-1046

Tel: (770) 913-9332
Fax: (770) 913-0822
Email: info@babygooroo.com
Website: babygooroo.com